JOAN OF ARC

Brian Williams

Designed by Kate Penoyre

Illustrated by Roger Payne

Ray Rourke Publishing Company, Inc.
Windermere, Florida 32786

Published by Ray Rourke Publishing Company, Inc.,
Windermere, Florida 32786.

Library of Congress Cataloging in Publication Data

Williams, Brian.
  Joan of Arc.

  SUMMARY: A biography of the peasant girl who led the
French army to victory against the English and paved
the way for the coronation of King Charles VII.
    1. Jeanne d'Arc, Saint, 1412-1431—Juvenile litera-
ture.   2. Orleans, France—Siege, 1428-1429—Juvenile
literature.   3. Christian saints—France—Biography—
Juvenile literature.   [1. Joan of Arc, Saint, 1412-1431.
2. Saints]   I. Payne, Roger, fl. 1969-   .   II. Title.
DC103.5.W49   1981   944'.026'0924   [B]   [92]   81-226
ISBN 0-86592-053-2   AACR1

JOAN OF ARC

In the early 1400s, a young peasant girl had a
vision that she, Joan of Arc, must drive the
English invaders from her beloved France.
She rallied the dispirited French army behind
the young king and saw him crowned.
The English captured her and burned her as a
witch. But they could not burn her spirit which
lives on in the hearts of those who worship
the Maid of Orleans as a saint.

Right: France in 1415.

Paris

lands recognizing Henry V

lands recognizing the Dauphin

Burgundian lands

4

France Divided

For nearly a century England and France had been locked in the bloody struggle we now call the Hundred Years' War. France was suffering. The English and their allies, the Burgundians, ruled much of the country. France's finest soldiers were dead. The Valois family (the royal house) was feeble. The King was insane, and his heir, Charles the Dauphin, was a coward.

The Battle of Agincourt, in 1415, looked like the beginning of the end for France. England's young warrior king, Henry V, had the country in his grasp. The English archers shot down the pride of French chivalry, yet the English suffered hardly any casualties themselves. Surely total defeat could not be far away. But three years before there had been born the war leader who was to save France – and that leader was a young girl. Joan of Arc was to bring the French new inspiration and drive out the English. She is her country's greatest heroine, and her story became a legend.

The Battle of Agincourt destroyed the flower of French chivalry. Afterwards, France was in the grip of Henry V, the young warrior king of England.

5

Voices at Domrémy

When Joan of Arc was born in 1412
France was a suffering and divided
nation. She was born at Domrémy, a
small village on the border between
the Duke of Burgundy's territory and
the Dauphin's lands. Domrémy was a
poor village, for the war had brought
trade to a standstill, and the villagers
lived in fear of bandits and Burgundian marauders. The only time Joan
left the village as a child was when her
family fled from a raid.

Her father, Jacques, was a farmer.
Joan had three brothers, and a sister
who died young. Joan's mother taught
her to sew and cook and to say the
Lord's Prayer. But she could not read

Joan and her visions were regarded with pride and awe by the villagers.

or write, although when she was older she did learn to sign her name.

Joan was a good daughter and worked hard, helping to herd her father's cattle. She was just like any other girl, until one summer's day, when she was 13. She was in the garden. Suddenly she saw a bright light and heard a voice. Joan believed the voice was that of God, for it told her to pray and lead a good life. Soon afterwards, she began to see visions. The villagers of Domrémy were amazed. For Joan told them she had seen three saints, St. Michael, St. Catherine, and St. Margaret. They had told her that she must leave home to perform a great task.

Joan was guided by her "voices" for the rest of her life. The people of Domrémy looked at Joan with awe – and pride. They came to consult her, to ask her to tell their fortunes. And she even visited the Duke of Lorraine at his castle.

Her parents, however, were anxious. When Joan refused to marry a young man who asked for her hand, they were angry. Joan explained that her voices had told her she must never marry. By the time she was 16 she had tried to run away several times. She told her father that she had been entrusted by God with a sacred mission. She must go to the aid of the Dauphin and save France.

Joan's party rode for many nights before they saw the walls of Chinon.

Joan's Mission

Joan knew that the Dauphin and his
court were at Chinon. How could she
get there and speak with him? She
traveled to Vaucouleurs, the nearest
Valois stronghold, to see the garrison
commander, Robert de Baudricourt.
She told him about her voices, but de
Baudricourt refused to take her
seriously. He sent her home.

Secretly, de Baudricourt feared that
Joan might be a witch. In medieval
Europe people were quick to blame

magic and sorcery for any unusual happening. So he was suspicious of this girl and her "voices".

When Joan came to see him for a third time, de Baudricourt was prepared. A priest accompanied him, wearing a cloak blessed with holy water. If Joan were a witch, the priest explained, she would fall back in terror from the cloak. If she were truly good, she would approach without fear. Joan was summoned. And at once she fell on her knees before the priest, asking his blessing.

Reassured, de Baudricourt listened as Joan told him what her voices had commanded. She was to raise the siege of Orléans. Then, she was to take the Dauphin to Rheims and see him crowned King of France.

De Baudricourt shook his head sadly. He had spent the whole winter struggling to defend Vaucouleurs and he feared that the Dauphin was close to defeat. Orléans was besieged by an English army. If the city fell, the enemy would seize all the Valois lands in the south. Already he had heard that the Dauphin's cowardly advisers were urging him to give up and flee to Spain or Scotland.

What possible chance did this 16-year-old girl have of turning defeat into victory? Still, there seemed little harm in sending her to Chinon. De Baudricourt gave Joan an escort of six men and dressed her in men's clothes as a disguise.

To reach the Dauphin the little party had to cross enemy territory, so they traveled mostly by night. The journey took 11 days. One of Joan's companions later recalled: "We were all afraid, but Joan told us not to be, for God would take care of us".

Eluding the English sentries, they reached the Loire river, and found a small boat to take them across to Chinon. Above the little town loomed the massive castle. Only within stone walls did Charles the Dauphin feel safe.

The Standard is Raised

De Baudricourt had sent a messenger to Chinon to tell the Dauphin about Joan and her miraculous voices. Her arrival worried the indecisive Charles. For two days he refused to see her.

When at last he summoned her into the great hall, he hid among the assembled courtiers to see if Joan would recognize him. She had never seen the Dauphin before. Yet she went up to him boldly and told him that he was "the true son of the old king and rightful heir to the throne of France".

Charles was impressed. He was eager to believe in Joan and her voices. At the same time, however, he was terrified of offending the Church. For if Joan's voices came not from God but from the Devil, the Church might declare her a heretic. Charles handed her over to the priests at Poitiers University to be questioned. The priests found no harm in Joan and reported favorably to Charles.

To Joan, the next move was quite simple. They must march to raise the siege of Orléans. That done, they would go to Rheims and there Charles would be crowned. Success at Orléans would prove that her voices were real.

With fresh heart, the soldiers prepared. Joan was given a suit of armor and the personal retainers of a knight – two pages and a squire. Her special standard showed Jesus blessing a fleur de lys (France's national emblem) held by the angels Michael and Gabriel. She was given a white warhorse to ride and practiced with a lance in the castle tiltyard. She announced that her sword lay in the church of St. Catherine of Fierbois – and a sword was found there, hidden behind the altar.

Soldiering came naturally to Joan. Two of the Dauphin's bravest knights, Etienne la Vignolles (known as La Hire) and Jean, Duke of Alençon, became Joan's firm friends. And her brothers, Jean and Pierre, came from Domrémy to join the army as it set off for Orléans. On Joan's orders, there was to be no drunkenness or swearing, for the men were now God's soldiers. She sent a message to the English. It read: "Leave France or I shall make you go away, whether you will or not".

Joan took her leave of the
Dauphin and led the French
army to raise the siege of
Orléans.

15

The Relief of Orléans

Orléans had been under attack since the autumn of 1428. It was vital to the Dauphin's cause, a strategic and strongly fortified city.

The English had surrounded Orléans. During the winter they had captured several outer defense posts. They occasionally bombarded the city with cannon fire from a ring of forts.

Despite the siege the French could go in and out of Orléans, by boat or through a northern gate which they had managed to keep open. The countryside was so ravaged that there was little food. Joan set out with supplies of food and gunpowder and several hundred fresh troops.

Inspired by Joan, the French stormed the English forts. Right: Joan's victory ride into the city.

The commander of Orléans rode boldly through the English lines to welcome Joan. The supplies were loaded into boats and the entire relief force, with its horses, crossed the river under the noses of the English forts.

The arrival of help put fresh hope into the people of Orléans. They crowded the streets for a glimpse of Joan. More French troops arrived, and on May 4 Joan led her men against the English forts. Inspired by her courage, the French crossed the river and stormed the bastions. The fighting was furious and Joan was struck by an arrow. Her men faltered until, with her wound bandaged, she returned to lead them.

The English were so surprised by the sudden French onslaught that they were driven into the river, where many of their knights drowned. They retreated, but Joan would not allow the French to pursue them because it was Sunday.

She re-entered the city in triumph. Soon all France would hear of the "Maid of Orléans".

The Battle of Patay

Joan's exploits at Orléans caused a great stir. Believing that God was on their side, the French were prepared to fight as never before. Soldiers and courtiers alike were struck by Joan's honesty and simplicity. She ate little, drank little, and spoke little; she loved to talk with the soldiers but hated meetings and crowds. She looked cheerful, but often wept. Untrained in warfare, she gave orders as calmly as a veteran commander.

While the French marveled at Joan, the English began to hate the sound of her name. They were convinced that she must have used "false enchantments and sorcery" to beat them. She must be a witch.

Joan did not stay in Orléans for the celebrations. She rode to see the Dauphin at Tours, and urged him to go at once to Rheims. As usual Charles did not know what to do. His courtiers advised him to proceed with caution.

Charles decided to advance along the Loire valley, capturing towns one by one, rather than risk a dash northward to Rheims. Joan was disappointed, but pleased that her friend, the Duke of Alençon, was to command the French army.

The English, meanwhile, were trying to reorganize. An army of 5000 had been assembled by Lord Talbot and Sir John Fastolf. On June 18, 1429, the advancing French came upon the English at the village of Patay.

Although they had a larger army, the French hesitated. Perhaps they

remembered Agincourt. This gave Fastolf and his Burgundian allies time to withdraw, leaving Talbot and his men to fight a rearguard action. Joan was furious. "You will need good spurs to catch the English," she told the Duke of Alençon.

However, Patay was no second Agincourt. The English had chosen a weak defensive position, and the French cavalry rode in on them from

both flanks while the infantry attacked the English center. It was a massacre. Almost 2000 English were killed or captured, while the French lost hardly a man.

Lord Talbot himself was among the prisoners. He was a valuable prize, for the more important a captive, the higher the price demanded as a ransom for his release. While the French counted their ransom money, the English retreated northward. Their garrisons fled from the Loire valley, and the road to Rheims at last lay open.

The French cavalry charged the English lines from both flanks.

Coronation at Rheims

Joan did not fight with the French army at the Battle of Patay. She had remained with the Dauphin, trying to shake him into action. So far he had taken little part in the war.

Joan was all for making a forced march to capture Paris before their enemies had time to recover. Charles refused. He thought it too dangerous. But he was finally persuaded to go to Rheims for his coronation.

In June 1429 the army gathered at Gien. From all over the countryside men came to fight for Joan and the Dauphin. As they marched to Rheims, towns once loyal to the English and Burgundians surrendered and swore allegiance to Charles.

At Troyes, the citizens closed the gates and prepared to fight. They had heard terrible stories of Joan, the "witch of Orléans" and were too frightened to let her enter. They sent a priest named Brother Richard to parley with her. Trembling, he approached Joan, sprinkling holy water in front of him. She burst out laughing. "Come closer," she smiled, "I won't disappear". Brother Richard told the citizens that Joan was no witch. And, seeing that they were surrounded anyway, the good people of Troyes surrendered.

On July 16 the army entered Rheims. The coronation took place next day. The Dauphin's seven-year wait was over. He was now Charles VII, King of France. Joan knelt before him, weeping tears of joy, and called him her king for the first time.

The English had suffered a heavy blow. As the news spread, more towns swore allegiance to Charles. The English retreated to their strongholds in Normandy, while the Duke of Burgundy pondered his next move.

Peace seemed near and Joan dreamed of returning home. Charles asked her what reward she would like for her services. All Joan asked was that from now on the villagers of Domrémy should pay no more taxes. For herself, she wanted nothing.

Once Charles was anointed with the holy oil, he was the lawful King of France. It was treason for any man to rebel against him. Joan stood close by during the solemn ceremony. She kept her banner beside her. "It deserves the honor, she said proudly. Her parents were in the congregation, watching. They had traveled from Domrémy at public expense.

Outside the Walls of Paris

Paris, the key to final victory, remained in enemy hands. Instead of attacking the city, Charles set off on a tour of his kingdom. Joan was dismayed.

Charles would not listen to her. He was holding secret peace talks with the Duke of Burgundy (who held Paris) and hoped to win the city by cunning. Joan was unconvinced. She did not like or understand diplomacy. The English would have to be defeated in battle before they would make peace.

In August Charles decided to return south to the Loire valley. The people of Rheims feared that their new King was abandoning them. Joan was relieved to learn that an English army had cut off Charles' retreat. Now they would have to attack Paris.

Though badly wounded, Joan still called out encouragement to her soldiers. But it was too late. Charles used her wound as an excuse to declare a truce, and lost the chance of victory.

Joan and the Duke of Alençon led the army north, while Paris hurriedly prepared to meet the attack. People barricaded the city gates and their houses. Cannon were hauled into position along the ramparts and tubs of stones made ready to repair breaches in the city walls.

The French built a bridge of boats across the Seine river and, with Joan at their head, rushed to attack the St. Honoré gate. Ladders were set up against the walls, and bundles of sticks thrown in the ditches to bridge them.

Joan showed reckless courage. Her standard-bearer fell dead beside her and she herself was wounded in the thigh. As she was carried from the fight she cried out to her soldiers to press on. But it was too late. Charles made a cease-fire agreement with the Duke of Burgundy. Sadly, the French buried their dead and turned their backs on Paris. It was a bitter blow to retreat, leaving the Burgundian flags still flying over the city.

In fact Charles had been tricked. The Duke was merely buying time, while he and his English allies prepared for war again. The French had lost their chance of a swift victory.

Back at Gien, the army disbanded. Joan wanted to go with the Duke of Alençon, to plan a new campaign against the English in Normandy, but Charles refused to let her go. Together Joan and Alençon were too powerful. Better to keep them apart.

Joan accompanied the King to Bourges. Her voices were silent and she was downcast. Why had things begun to go wrong?

Capture at Compiègne

To console Joan for the failure at Paris, the King offered to ennoble her family. Her brothers Jean and Pierre accepted, taking the knightly name du Lis. But Joan refused. She remained simply Joan or *La Pucelle* (The Maid). Her father called himself Jacques Darc, but Joan was never known as Jeanne d'Arc (Joan of Arc) during her lifetime.

In the winter of 1429–30 Joan led some minor raids and an unsuccessful siege. Spring came and Charles realized how he had been deceived, for the Duke of Burgundy was preparing to attack Compiègne. Rheims and the other towns loyal to the Valois cause were also threatened. Worse still, Charles learned that the boy-king of England, Henry VI, had landed in France. The English hoped to crown Henry King of France at Rheims.

Joan promised the citizens of the loyal towns that she would defend them. During Easter she was thoughtful. Her voices had spoken again; they had told her she would soon be a prisoner. But she kept her word, and rode off to save Compiègne.

Joan and her small force entered the town by night and next morning they raided the Burgundian camp. Riding back, they ran into an English ambush. The gates of Compiègne had to be slammed shut before the last riders were safe inside. The French rearguard was surrounded and Joan was dragged from her horse.

Joan was a prisoner of John of Luxembourg, who was anxious not to lose her. Fearing that the French would try to rescue Joan, he sent her to his castle. There she was treated kindly by John's wife, who begged Joan to dress like a woman again. For she knew the English wanted to burn Joan as a witch because she wore men's clothes.

Joan tried twice to escape. First she attempted to have herself smuggled

out in a large bundle of firewood. Then, in despair, she jumped from a high window and fell into the moat.

The English sent Pierre Cauchon, Bishop of Beauvais, to bargain with the Burgundians. The Bishop had been driven from his lands by the French. He hated Joan: in his eyes she was an enemy of the Church.

He offered the Burgundians 10,000 gold crowns for Joan, and they accepted. In January 1431 she was hurriedly moved to Rouen. Here, in English-held Normandy, she was beyond all hope of rescue. Yet, while Joan's loyal soldiers grieved, King Charles made no effort to help her. He did not even make an offer of ransom for her freedom. It seems that he was glad to be rid of her.

Locked out of the city in the confusion, Joan was pulled from her horse by a Burgundian archer.

Trial at Rouen

Joan's captors hated and feared her. This was not simply because she had beaten them in battle. She was accused of heresy and witchcraft. And in the Middle Ages these crimes were punishable by death.

It suited the English to have Joan tried by the Church. They wanted to prove that Charles was in league with the Devil. By burning Joan, they could ruin the French cause – or so they thought.

Joan's trial began in the Chapel Royal at Rouen Castle. Her judges were Bishop Cauchon and Jean le Maitre, Vice Inquisitor of France. The Inquisitor's job was to hunt out heretics and persuade them (often by torture) to confess their "sins" and return to the teachings of the Church.

After more than six months in prison, Joan looked pale and ill. Nevertheless, she defended herself well, giving calm, common-sense answers to Cauchon's questions. But certain matters, she insisted, must remain secret. Her voices said so.

Joan knew she was on trial for her life. But she could only speak the truth. Her honest replies sealed her fate.
Left: As the executioner set light to the faggots, an English soldier gave Joan a wooden cross.

Cauchon replied that she must obey the Church in all things, including her dress. (Joan still wore men's clothes.) The questions went on and on, day after day. What language did Joan's saints use? Answer: French. Was St. Michael naked? At this Joan laughed out loud. "Do you think God cannot afford to clothe him?" she retorted.

Yet she could never forget that she was on trial for her life. On May 24 she was taken to a cemetery where a scaffold had been set up. The list of her "sins" was read aloud and, when Cauchon threatened her with burning, Joan broke down in tears. She agreed to obey the Church and wear women's clothes. Perhaps she hoped to go free. But the English told her she would spend the rest of her life in prison.

When she heard this, Joan withdrew her "confession". She dressed in rough men's clothes and boldly repeated her belief that her voices came from heaven.

Cauchon showed no mercy. On May 30 Joan was taken to the market place and burned at the stake. As the fire was lit, an Englishman in the crowd handed her a little wooden cross on the end of a stick.

While the fire still blazed, the faggots were pulled aside so that all could see that the Maid of Orléans was really dead. Even some of the watching English wept, and Henry VI's secretary wrote: "We are all lost, for we have burnt a good and holy person".

When it was all over, the executioner found Joan's heart still uncharred. He was told to throw it into the Seine with her ashes. The English wanted to hear no more of the Maid of Orléans.

France's Heroine

Six months after Joan's death the 10-year-old Henry VI of England was crowned King of France – but at Paris, not Rheims. Bishop Cauchon took part in the ceremony. The coronation was no more than an empty gesture, for Joan's inspiration had turned the tide of war in favor of France. The English Regent, a capable ruler, died in 1435, and after this the English hold on France weakened steadily. Henry VI was a weak king and the Burgundians – seeing the way the war was going – abandoned him and made peace with Charles. In 1437 Charles at last entered Paris. By 1450 Normandy itself, so long an English stronghold, was in French hands.

In 1450 King Charles ordered an inquiry into Joan's trial – and in 1456 a commission set up by the Pope declared that she was innocent of heresy. A great celebration feast was held at Orléans, where Joan's courage had changed the course of the war.

Charles died in 1461. His successor, King Louis XI, signed a treaty with England in 1475. The Hundred Years' War was over, and France was united.

Joan had not lived to see the victory she had earned. But she was not forgotten. Many people claimed she was not dead at all, and for years there were rumors that she had escaped from Rouen. There were several false "Joans", and the most skillful imposter even convinced one of Joan's brothers for a while.

Stories of Joan's deeds passed into legend and there were wild tales about her identity. One said that she was really of royal blood, and another that she led an "underground" witch cult. But most people today admire her as she appeared to her followers: as a peasant girl who believed God had called her, and whose faith in her "voices" was never shaken.

As the years passed, Joan of Arc became France's national heroine. Napoleon put up a statue of her in Orléans, declaring that she symbolized France's unity in time of danger. In 1920 she was canonized by the Roman Catholic Church, and became St. Joan. June 24 is a French national holiday in her honor; but Joan is admired and loved all over the world.

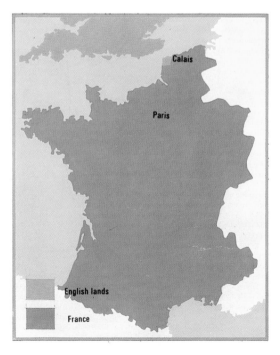

Above: France at the end of the Hundred Years' War.

Important Dates

1403	Charles the Dauphin born
1411	Civil war begins between Burgundians and Armagnacs (supporters of the Orléans family)
1412	Joan born
1413	Henry V becomes King of England
1415	Henry V invades France and defeats the French at Agincourt
1418	Burgundians capture Paris
1419	Murder of John the Fearless, Duke of Burgundy, probably by the Dauphin
1420	Treaty of Troyes: Henry V acknowledged as heir to the French throne, marries Charles VI's daughter, Catherine
1422	Deaths of Henry V of England and Charles VI of France
1424	John, Duke of Bedford, regent for Henry VI of England, defeats the French at Verneuil
1428	English begin siege of Orléans Joan visits Vaucouleurs

1429	February: Joan at Chinon May: Joan relieves Orléans June: Battle of Patay July: Coronation of Charles VII September: French attack Paris (unsuccessfully)
1430	May: Joan captured at Compiègne by the Burgundians, later handed over to the English
1431	January: Joan's trial begins at Rouen May: Execution of Joan
1435	Burgundians and French make peace – the Peace of Arras Death of the Duke of Bedford, Regent of England
1436	Charles VII wins Paris
1449	French capture Rouen
1453	Battle of Castillon England's only possession in France is Calais Henry VI becomes insane
1456	Joan is declared innocent of all the charges brought against her
1475	Hundred Years' War ends
1553	English lose Calais
1920	Joan is canonized and becomes St. Joan.